The Propaganda Bureau

ISBN 978-1481236133
Printed by Createspace

THE PROPAGANDA BUREAU

Andrew Montford

Summary

In 2007, the BBC Trust announced that a seminar of the 'best scientific experts' had decided that climate science was settled and that dissenting voices no longer deserved equal treatment.

It has recently been revealed that the seminar was attended mainly by green activists. Only three scientists attended and only two with expertise in climate science.

Of the 28 attendees only one might have been expected to take a dissenting view on climate issues.

The seminar was part of a series, funded by green activists and others and attended by senior BBC decision-makers.

The seminars were intended to influence all of the BBC's output, bringing green storylines into everything from science to comedy. There is strong evidence that this aim was achieved.

The BBC has spent enormous sums of money trying to prevent the seminar attendees being identified, using a team of six lawyers, including two barristers, to prevent a lone pensioner from obtaining the information under FOI.

When the BBC's refusal to identify the attendees under FOI was challenged via the Information Commissioner, a hitherto unnoticed public document that revealed the identities was redacted. This was done at the instigation of one of the seminar's co-organisers.

The seminar series was originally authorised by the then head of news, Tony Hall (now the new director-general of the BBC, Lord Hall).

There are links between the seminar series and other scandals, such as Climategate and the 2011 revelation that the BBC had been accepting free programming from green activist groups.

The leaked email

In October 2007, while looking for something interesting to read, I came across a blog posting about a leaked BBC email. While it was interesting, it appeared relatively insignificant. There was no hint that this was to be the beginning of an investigation that would span more than five years and to lead to one of the greatest scandals in the history of the BBC.

The email in question had been sent by the corporation's environment reporter Roger Harrabin and appeared to show that he had been trying to develop a party line for his colleagues in the wake of a recent setback to the green movement. A few weeks earlier, the High Court in the UK had ruled that Al Gore's global warming movie *An Inconvenient Truth* contained major errors and the judge had stipulated that it could therefore only be used in schools with strong caveats about its factual accuracy. At the time, there were attempts to have the movie shown in every school in the country and so the court's decision was a major defeat for environmental campaigners.

Harrabin's response had been to try to ensure that the central tenets of the global warming campaign remained safe from the fallout from the court's decision, while accepting some limited criticism of the Gore movie. As he said in the email

> In any future reporting of Gore we should be careful not to suggest that the High Court says Gore was wrong on climate.

> We might say something like: 'Al Gore whose film was judged by the High Court to have used some debatable science' or 'Al Gore whose film was judged in the High Court to be controversial in parts'.

> The key is to avoid suggesting that the judge disagreed with the main climate change thesis.

3

The email gave a remarkable insight into the inner workings of the BBC and flew in the face of claims by senior BBC staff that they had no 'line' on climate change.

At around the same time, I had been looking into Harrabin's work myself, having been appalled at the bias in his journalism. My research, which was at an early stage, had revealed little of interest, apart from Harrabin's profile page on the website of BBC Radio's flagship *Today* programme, where he was a frequent contributor. Although this was mostly just boilerplate, the page referred to Harrabin being co-director of something called the Cambridge Media and Environment Programme (CMEP), an organisation which apparently tried to find ways to engage the media on stories about 'sustainable development'. (The page actually incorrectly referred to the 'Cambridge Environment and Media Programmes', but it was clearly the same organisation.) There were almost no other details, apart from the fact that Harrabin's activities were part-funded by the BBC, with the rest coming from unnamed private sources. I was struck at the time by how odd it was that the BBC would be using public money to persuade itself to engage on environmental issues. Everything seemed to be back to front. As I said to my blog readers at the time:

> Doesn't it seem stranger still that the loot is being sent to an organisation run by one of its own employees? This seems to reverse the normal employer/employee relationship. Shouldn't the higher-ups at the BBC be telling Harrabin what to do?
>
> And isn't it yet more bizarre that it is trying to promote inclusion of particular issues in the news agenda – an overtly political act if ever there was one? The BBC, remember, has no line on climate change (and presumably the whole question of environmentalism too). Is the BBC actually fund-

ing a campaign to promote environmentalism on the airwaves?

I don't know about you, but I smell fish.

Planet Relief

I thought no more of it. However, at the start of 2008, I was reading about the latest in a long line of environmental protests, coverage of which increasingly filled the airwaves. This latest event was 'eDay', in which people would be encouraged to switch off electrical appliances for a day. Irritated by the hype, I wondered who it was who was behind the hectoring and a little web browsing quickly took me to the source – an environmentalist named Matt Prescott. Prescott had recently qualified from Oxford with a degree in zoology, but already had a long track record in environmental campaigning.

One profile of him showed that he was involved in no fewer than eleven blogs, most with green themes. He had also organised something called the Oxford Earth Summit and in 2005 he had launched a campaign to ban incandescent light bulbs. He was remarkably well connected too, having worked for:

- Prof. Norman Myers (a British environmentalist)

- Sir Crispin Tickell,(a British diplomat, environmentalist and academic)

- George Monbiot, (journalist and environmentalist)

- Jon Plowman (head of BBC Comedy)

- Glenwyn Benson (controller of BBC Knowledge)

as well as Roger Harrabin.

His website also revealed that he had been involved at a senior level in another BBC green project called 'Planet Relief'. This was to have been a worldwide telethon to promote green causes and had been scheduled for January 2008. However, it had been cancelled shortly after the plans for the broadcast had been announced – senior BBC editors had met with a wall of criticism for putting the corporation's weight behind what appeared to be a naked piece of environmentalist propaganda.

With Prescott such a committed green campaigner, it was remarkable to see him at the head of a large BBC project, and doubly so when his youth and lack of broadcasting experience were also taken into account. In a blog post describing what I had found, I explained:

> The justification for the licence fee has always been that the BBC is objective and impartial, and yet here we have Mr Prescott brought in from outside, apparently to use public resources to promote his own (and presumably the BBC's) political views.

It was also very odd that Prescott said he had worked for Plowman, the head of BBC comedy; there was certainly no indication that Prescott had a background in comedy. However, there was in fact a straightforward explanation. Plowman had been a strong supporter of the Planet Relief effort too. In fact, as Prescott's website revealed, there was at least one other familiar name involved:

> Joe Smith (Open University) and Roger Harrabin (BBC News) also played a crucial role in helping to get things off the ground a couple of years ago.

In his blog post, Prescott explained that it had been Harrabin and Smith who had introduced him to Plowman. The meeting had apparently taken place in Cambridge 'a couple of years ago', an explanation that put the date some time in 2006.

The Sidney Sussex seminar

Harrabin's activities were starting to look very interesting and a little more research quickly confirmed my suspicions that something untoward was going on. I had spent a long time trying to find details of CMEP, but surprisingly it had no website of its own. However, there were a few details on websites run by other organisations. From these, I was able to work out that Joe Smith was also a director of CMEP, and that he and Harrabin had been responsible for organising a series of seminars on green issues for the BBC. One of these in particular looked to be important – the seminar held at Sidney Sussex College Cambridge, on September 14th and 15th 2006. The participants had apparently examined how non-factual program makers might include environmental and development issues in their storylines. The timescale was exactly right to be the occasion of the meeting with Plowman that Prescott had described on his webpage, and it also explained the strange alliance of the comedy producer and the green activist.

Amongst the information posted about the Sidney Sussex seminar was a list of attendees and this showed clearly that this was no meeting of junior staff. The names were very much a Who's Who of the movers and shakers in the upper echelons of the BBC. This, then, was remarkable. A fresh-faced PhD, not long out of Oxford, had somehow managed, over the course of no more than a year or two, to move into a position from which he was able to influence some of the most powerful people in the BBC. Moreover, it appeared that as a result of these meetings he had been able to land himself a major BBC project to co-ordinate. It was a remarkable story.

Some more thoughts occurred to me. Was Prescott a BBC employee or a consultant? If the former, was the position advertised openly, and if the latter, what particular expertise was Prescott supposed to bring in order to justify his retention? His website suggested that he was being employed by Roger Harrabin in some shape or form. Moreover, the fact that Harrabin had invited a rather wet-behind-the-ears environmentalist to meet such important people was also surely deserving of some explanation.

Harmless Sky

Later that year, another blogger started to become interested in CMEP and at last I was no longer investigating Harrabin and Smith alone. Tony Newbery is the host of the Harmless Sky blog, which he writes from his home in rural West Wales. Like me, Newbery had been appalled by the BBC's output on green matters and he had been particularly incensed by an interview given by the journalist Jeremy Paxman to the BBC's in-house magazine, *Ariel*, in 2007. Paxman said that the BBC had given up on any pretence of neutrality on the question of global warming, and although this was a statement that most sceptics would readily agree with, the fact that the corporation's bias could be admitted so freely without anything being done about it was infuriating.

Newbery's response had been to look into the BBC's official position on climate change and impartiality, and his research soon led him to a report published in June that same year by the corporation's governing body, the BBC Trust. Entitled 'From SeeSaw to Wagonwheel', and written by a former BBC journalist John Bridcut, this document explained some of the issues around the BBC's approach to impartiality – indeed, it was subtitled 'Safeguarding impartiality in the 21st century'. Buried deep within the report was a discussion of how BBC journalists would deal with the vexed question of climate change in future:

> The BBC has held a high-level seminar with some
> of the best scientific experts, and has come to the
> view that the weight of evidence no longer justi-
> fies equal space being given to the opponents of
> the consensus [on anthropogenic global warm-
> ing].

This appeared then to be a fairly frank explanation of how
the BBC had arrived at its current state of editorial bias. However, given the BBC's propensity for using activist scientists or
eco-campaigners in its broadcast output – typically describing both as 'climate change experts', Newbery had immediately been suspicious of who had been involved in this seminar of the 'best scientific experts' and he decided to try to
find out directly from the BBC.

Newbery's FOI request, sent in the middle of 2007, had
been wide-ranging, covering every conceivable aspect of the
seminar – times, places, attendees, the letter of invitation,
records and other transcripts. However, the BBC is notorious
for being evasive of Freedom of Information requests, having
managed to negotiate an opt-out from the Act for activities
related to journalism. The seminar was hardly journalism of
course, but nevertheless the corporation intended to inter-
pret the exemption very broadly, as they explained in their
response.

> In this case, the information you have requested
> is outside the scope of the Act because informa-
> tion relating to the seminar is held to help in-
> form the BBC's editorial policy around reporting
> climate change. The only exception to this is the
> logistic details which you have requested

> In this respect I can confirm that the seminar was
> called 'Climate Change – the Challenge to Broad-

casting' and was held at the BBC's Television Centre in White City London on 26 January 2006. The seminar ran from 9.30am to 5.30pm.

We are also happy to voluntarily provide you with some further information relating to the seminar.

The attendees at the seminar were made up of 30 key BBC staff and 30 invited guests who are specialists in the area of climate change. It was hosted by Jana Bennett, Director of Vision (then Television), BBC and Helen Boaden, Director of News BBC. It was chaired by Fergal Keane, Special Correspondent with BBC News. The seminar's key speaker was Robert McCredie, Lord May of Oxford.

Seminar had the following aims:

- To offer a clear summary of the state of knowledge on the issue
- To find where the main debates lie
- To invoke imagination to allow the media to deal with the scope of the issue
- To consider the BBC's role in public debate.

The details were tantalising. Lord May is well known in sceptic circles having been prominent in efforts to promote the global warming agenda in his roles as government chief scientist and later as president of the Royal Society.

With the BBC refusing to divulge much useful information about the seminars, Newbery appeared to have hit a dead-end. However, determined not to be beaten, he had resolved to see what he could find out from information in the public domain and he had sat down in front of his computer and started to investigate. It was not long before he struck gold in the shape of the website of the International Broadcasting Trust (IBT). This was the same site on which I had read of the Sidney Sussex seminar.

IBT is a lobbying group funded by a group of charities including many involved in the global warming debate, such as Friends of the Earth, Christian Aid, Oxfam and Tearfund. Their website explained:

> The International Broadcasting Trust (IBT) is an educational charity which seeks to promote high quality television and new media coverage on matters of international significance. IBT represents a coalition of international charities campaigning for high quality television coverage of matters of international significance or interest.

The idea of a charity campaigning for coverage of any set of issues on the airwaves was obviously intriguing, as it would immediately challenge the impartiality of any broadcaster that was receptive to these approaches. Some of the other details on the website were just as alarming.

> Our work focuses on four main areas of activity:
>
> - lobbying government, regulators and broadcasters
> - dialogue with the main public service broadcasters
> - research on television coverage of the developing world
> - developing a slate of innovative programme ideas

This appeared to suggest that the situation was even worse than it had first appeared – not only was the IBT campaigning for particular issues to be covered on television stations but was also delivering up fully fledged programming ideas. There was clearly a delicate line to be trodden for the broadcasters – between being receptive to suggestions from outside and being merely a conduit for the campaigns of others.

While Newbery had been concerned that the IBT might not be working in the public interest, it was one particular aspect of the group's work that intrigued him. This was a series of meetings that they had been organising with the BBC:

Real World Brainstorms

Background

The Real World Brainstorms take place annually and are co-hosted by BBC Vision and BBC News. The aim is to bring together key decision makers within broadcasting with a mix of writers, producers and environment and development specialists to explore how we can more effectively represent our interconnected world. Delegates exchange views on key issues and ideas, discussing fresh approaches to stories which impact here in the UK and around the world. Past seminars have had enormously positive feedback, inspiring major programme seasons as well as diverse individual projects. But the meetings are not about pitching ideas – they are about making space for fresh thinking about the way the world is and how it might be represented more richly. The seminars are organized jointly by the BBC, IBT and the Cambridge Media and Environment Programme.

At that point Newbery knew nothing of CMEP, so his attention was not drawn by the mention of it at the end of the paragraph. However, further down the page something else

had caught his attention – a description of one of the Real
World Brainstorms:

2006

A one day event was held in London on January
26 2006, focusing on climate change and its impact on development. The brainstorm brought
together 28 BBC executives and independent producers, this time including several from BBC News,
and 28 policy experts. It was chaired by Fergal
Keane and looked ahead to the next 10 years, to
explore the challenges facing television in covering this issue. Several delegates attended from
developing countries, including Ethiopia, China
and Bangladesh.

There could be little doubt that this was the same seminar
referred to in the BBC's FOI response – the details were almost identical. However, Newbery's sharp eyes had noticed
a critical difference between the Trust's description and the
IBT's. While the Trust had referred to a seminar of 'the best
scientific experts', the IBT spoke of '28 policy experts'. If the
conclusion of the seminar had been, as the Trust had explained, that sceptic views of global warming need no longer
be treated as equal, then policy experts were hardly the correct demographic to have made that assessment. And when
he checked back to the BBC's FOI response he had seen something that he had not originally noticed: the BBC had referred
to the seminar attendees as 'specialists in the area of climate
change', a description that was again somewhat different to
the Trust's version.

Like me, Newbery's interest had been piqued by the Cambridge and Media Environment Programme and, like me, he
struggled to find many details of their activities. But he was
able to find out a few fleeting references to CMEP on little

visited corners of the web. On the website called Earth Dialogues, he had found a page of biographies of the speakers and moderators at an environmental conference, among them Roger Harrabin.

Mr. Roger Harrabin

Environment Correspondent, British Broadcasting Corporation

Mr. Harrabin is environment correspondent for the BBC Radio 4 Today Programme, an associate Press Fellow of Wolfson College, Cambridge, and co-director of the Cambridge Media and Environment Programme – an organisation founded to engage media gate-keepers in debates on sustainable development. He has been reporting environment, transport, energy and development issues for the BBC for 17 years.

On another site Newbery had found some information about Joe Smith's involvement in CMEP. *The Great Global Warming Swindle* was a polemical television film that had attacked the credibility of mainstream climate science and had given huge publicity to dissenting views on global warming. It was inevitable that in the wake of the show's success that there would be a backlash and a few weeks later a 176-page complaint to the UK's broadcasting regulator OfCom was organised. This was a sophisticated effort, involving numerous signatories from among the great and the good of the scientific and environmental worlds and a webpage had been set up to publicise and coordinate the response. Among the biographies of those involved was that of Joe Smith:

Dr Joe Smith

Senior Lecturer in Environment at The Open University and Co-Director of the Cambridge Media and Environment Programme

Dr Smith peer reviewed the sections of the complaint relating to the media's coverage of climate change

'Within the protective bubble of media commissioning it is easy to see why Swindle looked like a good idea: it was provocative, naughty and counterintuitive. It gave voice to outcast experts, defied groupthink and surprised the audience. But pop the bubble, step outside and talk to the numerous and broad climate change science and policy community and it is viewed as one of the most unhelpful pieces of programme making about a science topic that anyone can remember. Britain had established itself as a leader in the extent and quality of public debate about climate change but the Swindle programme dented that. It is a clear example of how the media's desire to appear edgy and probing can leave everyone involved in a commission looking at best foolish and dated.'

As Newbery acidly noted at the time, Smith's views did not make him sound like an impartial and objective academic.

There was to be one last finding that had raised the curtain a little further on CMEP. The Tyndall centre is the UK's national centre for climate research and a paper on their website revealed the information that they had been funding CMEP as well as some details of the programme's work.

16. Tyndall supports media & environment programme

The Tyndall Centre is co-sponsoring the University of Cambridge Media and Environment Programme, run by Joe Smith (Open University) and Roger Harrebin [sic] (BBC) through the University of Cambridge's Committee for Interdisciplinary Environmental Studies (CIES). The Programme aims to overcome the obstacles to effective reporting of environment and sustainable development in the media, by bringing together about 15 media decision-makers (including news editors, producers and journalists) and a similar number of leading experts from the environmental research and policy community. The Tyndall Centre is co-sponsoring the Programme because we share its commitment to the effective communication of climate change information to increase knowledge and inspire discussion and debate in society. The Centre also places importance on the need to engage with the media to disseminate research results and other information relating to Tyndall activities, and sees the Programme as an excellent opportunity to build on links to this network.

The incredible disappearing Roger Harrabin

With Newbery and me both researching CMEP and publishing our results on our blogs, it was inevitable that our paths would cross eventually. The breakthrough came when Newbery read about my work on Matt Prescott and the CMEP seminars, and he immediately made the connection to his own work. However, as he read my article and followed the links, he unearthed something rather remarkable: our work on CMEP had not gone unnoticed – the profile of Harrabin that had appeared on the *Today* programme website had disappeared. This could have been coincidence, of course, but to make sure, I took a look at Matt Prescott's website as well. It was just as I had suspected: although the site was still there, the description of the meeting between Harrabin, Smith and Prescott at the Sidney Sussex conference had been slightly, but significantly, amended. All mention of Harrabin had been erased.

As I explained to my readers at the time, the original article read

> Joe Smith (Open University) and Roger Harrabin (BBC News) originally introduced me to Jon, in Cambridge, and also played a crucial role in helping to get things off the ground a couple of years ago.

Now it only said:

> Joe Smith (Open University) originally introduced me to Jon, in Cambridge, and also played a crucial role in helping to get things off the ground a couple of years ago.

Clearly this was no coincidence – only a few months had passed since I wrote my articles referring to the seminars. It seemed clear that there had been a coordinated attempt to hide Harrabin's involvement in the CMEP inquiries. We appeared to have unearthed something important.

Fortunately for us, Harrabin and Smith had reckoned without the availability of the Wayback Machine – a site that archives many, but not all pages on the web at regular intervals. By a stroke of good fortune, both the *Today* programme profile and Prescott's site appeared in the archive, and I was able to retrieve them as they originally were.

Another attendee

At the end of 2008, as commenters at both Newbery's blog and mine turned their minds to the question of the seminars, a few more details were unearthed from the depths of the web. One perceptive reader found what appeared to be a mention of the climate change seminar in a gossipy article in the *Times* in which journalist Rachel Johnson related a discussion with a Andrew Simms, a researcher at a left-wing thinktank called the New Economics Foundation.

> I asked Andrew Simms when he thought that the greens finally started preaching to the choir.
>
> 'Well, I thought that the piece Susie Watt did for Newsnight last week, questioning whether economic growth is good, was a real marker,' he said, 'But I think the real conversion took place about 18 months ago... when I was asked to attend a BBC seminar on climate change, and Fergal Keane was there.'

Johnson's article appeared at the end of January 2008, so the timing again appeared to match that of the BBC seminar, and with Keane's presence also matching the BBC's version of events there could be little doubt that this was the same event.

Simms was not a familiar name to anyone in the sceptic blogosphere but in fact, as well as his role at the New Economics Foundation, where he headed the climate change programme, he has also been on the boards of Greenpeace UK and the controversial 10:10 climate change campaign, and well as co-authoring a book with Smith entitled *Do Good Lives Have to Cost the Earth?* One reviewer had described the book as 'an eloquent and persuasive account of modern corporate greed, and how and why we should resist it'. It was therefore quite clear that Simms in no way matched the BBC Trust's description of 'the best scientific experts'. In fact it was hard to see him as in any way suitable for assessing the question of BBC impartiality on climate change.

Northern light

A few days after Simms had been identified as one of the attendees we made another significant breakthrough, which enabled us to settle the question of whether the attendees at the climate change seminar had been, as the BBC Trust had put it, 'the best scientific experts', or whether they were in fact policy experts, as the IBT had claimed. Another commenter at Newbery's blog had noted that the writer and political commentator Richard D North had written a brief account of his attendance at a meeting at BBC Television Centre that looked, yet again, as if it was the climate change seminar. Since North was known to have something of a contrarian streak we assumed that he might well be receptive to an approach and Newbery fired off a short email asking if he could tell us a little bit about the seminar. Fortunately, North was happy to talk and his response was devastating:

> I did attend the BBC climate change seminar and my impression is that it was part of the ongoing efforts by Roger Harrabin (environment analyst at the BBC) to help the corporation wrestle with the problem of balance and impartiality and robust reporting of the climate change debate.

> I think Roger Harrabin has not been a good reporter or analyst of climate change. He is not the worst by any means, but he has in my view missed many tricks. However, he has been serious if not very effective (actually often rather poor) in tackling the nature of the debate itself.

> By the way, my own view is that the biggest media failure has been in discussing the policy response to the science of climate change. I mean that though the discussion of the science has been bad the discussion of the policy response has been mostly abysmal. The BBC is only the worst of the

offenders on this score because (a) they are paid to be the best and (b) their efforts have fallen so far short of their stated ambitions in this area.

I found the seminar frankly shocking. The BBC crew (senior executives from every branch of the corporation) were matched by an equal number of specialists, almost all (and maybe all) of whom could be said to have come from the 'we must support Kyoto' school of climate change activists.

So far as I can recall I was alone in being a climate change sceptic (nothing like a denier, by the way) on both the science and policy response.

I was frankly appalled by the level of ignorance of the issue which the BBC people showed. I mean that I heard nothing that made me think any of them read any broadsheet newspaper coverage of the topic (except maybe the Guardian and that lazily). Though they purported to be aware that this was an immensely important topic, it seemed to me that none of them had shown even a modicum of professional journalistic curiosity on the subject. I am not saying that I knew what they all knew or thought, but I can say that I spent the day discussing the issue and don't recall anyone showing any sign of having read anything serious at all.

As you know the BBC has come to the conclusion that 'balance' cannot mean giving equal time to opposing views if one set of views is scientific and the opposing view is, so to speak, unscientific. I agree, and I see this sort of problem arises with MMR, GM, animal experimentation and lots of other topics. I do see it's a profound problem.

But the policy response to climate change is much more easy to discuss and the BBC like most broadcast media mostly fails at it. I could write more on this of course, but it may be useful just to say that broadcasters mostly balk at noting that it is incredibly unlikely that the current generation of leaders and citizens will do more that make a few faltering policy steps along what may one day develop into a low-carbon economy. Insofar as we do, it will be because action turned out to be cheap and convenient. Also, energy price volatility is likely to be a bigger immediate driver than climate change.

I argued at the seminar that I thought most broadcasting coverage on climate change was awful. But I also said there was no need for them to become self-conscious about it. This was because, though the issues were scientifically, politically and economically difficult, the BBC's reporting of the thing would improve as soon as their audience was asked to vote or pay for climate change policy. Ordinary realities and recognisable journalistic tensions would kick in and the corporation would give up its rather feeble activist propaganda. In short, they might never get their brain round the issue, but their ordinary journalistic habits would see them through once there was good old fashioned argument about spending money or effort on sorting the climate out – or failing to.

Of course my nose was out of joint. I was struck by the way my views were of only passing interest to the BBC and I have never been asked to aid their internal discussions since. It may be that they are spoiled for choice when it comes to intelligent, well-informed, sceptical voices to deliver a counter-intuitive challenge to their orthodoxies. I should say that I am not at all complaining that I'm not used on-air much. I mean only that the whole apparatus of self-examination on climate change policy seems really to have looked remarkably like subtle propaganda for the orthodoxies it was meant to interrogate.

There was plenty to disagree with in North's email, but it was now quite certain that the Trust had misled the public by telling them that scientists had been involved. Everybody else seemed quite certain that the attendees were at best policy people working in the area or, at worst, green activists. Whether the Trust had themselves been misled about the seminar or whether they were deliberately misleading the public was difficult to tell.

North's emails meant that 2008 had closed on a positive note. With strong evidence that the BBC Trust had misled the public about the seminar (perhaps inadvertently) and also an eyewitness to prove the point, it now looked as if we would be able to make our case to the BBC Trust and demand an investigation. Little did we realise, however, that the next three years would be characterised by frustration and anger as Harrabin, Smith, the BBC executive and the BBC Trust all resolutely refused to hear what we had to say.

Starting at the end of 2008 we launched a series of Freedom of Information requests, seeking more information on the seminars. The BBC, as expected, invoked its 'journalistic purposes' exemption to the FOI Act to resist attempts to get details of how much money it had put into CMEP. Our requests for internal and external correspondence, including Harrabin's emails to Smith, were also refused. Before long we were into the arduous process of appealing the BBC's decisions to the Information Commissioner (ICO).

Meanwhile we also attacked the problem from the other end, requesting Joe Smith's correspondence with Harrabin from the Open University. Here the response was more interesting, with the Open University arguing that Smith's activities at CMEP were private, and had nothing to do with the university. They claimed, rather surprisingly, that the seminars had not been funded by them, either in cash or in kind. By a stroke of good fortune, however, we were able to show that this response was not entirely true. In the small print of an academic paper Smith had written in the journal *Risk Analysis*, he thanked the Open University for providing transcription services for one of the seminars. So it looked as if the university had provided funding in kind, if not in cash. There followed a long battle to get the transcripts of this seminar. Smith first argued that these were private information, but when it looked as if the ICO was going to force their release, the story changed, with Smith claiming that he had been mistaken and that the transcripts had actually been lost. In the end, the university was forced to recreate the transcripts from the original audio recordings, but the results were disappointing – the new transcript appeared to have been put together in a way that made the meaning as hard to discern as possible and with a great deal of redaction. Names of attendees and even of their institutions had been removed, making any deduction of who had been involved impossible.

We tried other approaches too. One idea was to create an FOI request for the contents of the visitor book at BBC Television Centre. This time the BBC's response was that paper copies were destroyed after three months and that they did not hold any electronic copies. It was another dead-end.

Only a few of details we extracted under FOI were of use. We were able to get hold of some of the invoices for CMEP's funding, including those for the Tyndall Centre's contributions. The centre had put in £15,000, spread over three years. We noted that the first invoices had been issued by

Cambridge University, where CMEP was then based, while the final invoice had been raised on plain paper by CMEP itself, with the address given as Smith's home in Cambridge.

Another source of CMEP's funding was Defra, the UK government's environment ministry, and it seemed reasonable that they might have had someone in attendance at the seminar. Newbery therefore issued a further FOI request to try to identify the individual involved. As expected, Defra resisted, arguing that because of the number of reorganisations they had been involved in since the time of the seminar, it would cost too much to locate the information we wanted. However, in due course they passed on a message from Smith himself asking Newbery to get in touch. The email that eventually arrived from Smith was very much as expected, with a complete rejection of North's recollection of the seminar:

> I'm afraid I don't agree with [North's] account
> – indeed his presence [was] a reflection of the
> wide range of views on environmental change
> that were present!

However, he refused to give details of who had been in attendance, claiming that the seminars were held under the Chatham House rule. This was an interesting argument, since the Chatham House rule is normally understood only to prevent attribution of something that was said at a meeting, and indeed it was relatively straightforward to confirmed this from the website of Chatham House itself:

> **Can participants in a meeting be named as long as what is said is not attributed?**
> It is important to think about the spirit of the Rule. For example, sometimes speakers need to be named when publicizing the meeting. The Rule is more about the dissemination of the information after the event – nothing should be

done to identify, either explicitly or implicitly, who said what.

When pressed to confirm the BBC Trust's description of 'the best scientific experts', Smith appeared keen to give the impression that he did, but close examination suggests that his response was worded with lawyerly care.

> ...we agree with any suggestion that the meeting convened top scientific expertise, but this does not fully represent the fact that the meeting also included well informed business and policy community figures. It is in the nature of a huge and complex topic such as climate change that with having 15 or so specialists present from science, policy and business you inevitable [sic] have a wide range of views.

In fact, his reply could, on one reading, be completely consistent with a seminar at which Lord May, a committed environmental campaigner and a former board member of WWF, was the single scientist present. In these circumstances Smith's wording would also have been consistent with North's recollection.

The BBC Science Review

By the start of January 2010, the Information Commissioner had upheld the BBC's decision to withhold details of the seminar and Harrabin's correspondence with Smith. However, we were determined not to be beaten and in due course we appealed the ICO's decision to the Information Tribunal, the quasi-judicial body that is the next step in the appeal process. We had been aware for some time that the scope of the BBC's journalistic purposes exemption from FOI was the subject of another protracted legal process on unrelated matters.

A London solicitor named Steven Sugar had been trying to obtain a copy of a BBC editorial report on the corporation's coverage of the Israel–Palestine conflict, and his request had been refused, like ours, on the grounds of the journalistic purposes exemption. Sugar was well ahead of us by that point, with his appeal having reached the House of Lords. It was clear to Newbery and me that if Sugar won his case then the BBC would probably have to release the information we requested.

Meanwhile, at the start of the year there was another important development. On 6 Jan 2010 the chairman of the BBC Trust's Editorial Standards Committee, Richard Tait, announced a review of the impartiality of the corporation's science coverage. This sounded ominous, particularly since the press release announcing the inquiry made it clear that climate change was one of the areas that the inquiry would consider. We felt sure that the review would be used as an opportunity to sideline sceptics still further.

There were few other details – the press release did not reveal who would be running the inquiry and how submissions could be made. Nevertheless it was clearly going to be important for us to make ourselves heard. In particular, the story of CMEP was one which would have to be considered if the inquiry were to properly assess the BBC's coverage of global warming. We decided that the constructive approach would be to write to Tait asking that we be heard, and shortly afterwards we dispatched a letter to this end, although at that point we did not explain the details of our complaint.

A month later, we had heard nothing, and Newbery decided to apply some pressure. On 7 April 2010 he wrote to Bruce Vander, the Secretary of the Editorial Standards Committee, asking for confirmation that Tait had received our letter. A reply was received shortly afterwards, which said that the letter would be 'shared' with Tait and with the chairman of the inquiry, now revealed as the geneticist Professor Steve Jones. The wording of the reply suggested a certain evasiveness, so Newbery wrote again asking for confirmation that Tait had actually received the letter. This time Vander did not deign to reply, and by the end of the month Newbery felt forced to push harder. In a third letter he told Vander that he would be forced to take the matter up with the BBC Trust if Vander would not confirm that the letter had actually been received by Tait. The reply from Vander was polite but was again evasive – he would only say that a colleague had undertaken to 'share' the letter with Tait. Further letters went without a response, until finally at the start of June, Vander wrote once more:

> I am writing to confirm that your letter has been shared with Richard Tait.

While this bureaucratic obstructionism was infuriating, our efforts may actually have had the desired effect. Towards the end of April, I chanced upon a blog that discussed the BBC review of science coverage and pointed to an obscure page on the BBC website where submissions to the inquiry were being solicited. Perhaps we would get to have a say after all.

Over the summer Newbery started work on the submission, although there were distractions in the shape of the Climategate inquiries and families and holidays. However, at the end of June, there were some more interesting developments. Firstly the House of Lords referred the Sugar case back to the Court of Appeal and we were able to study where Sugar's case now stood. Among the details of the rulings of the lower courts we saw that there was still hope for our FOI cases before the Information Tribunal. The rulings of the lower courts had determined that at some point BBC information would no longer be held for journalistic purposes, but instead would be held for archival purposes – the scope of the journalistic purposes exemption was therefore rather narrower than had previously been thought. These rulings seemed to have passed muster with the House of Lords who now passed the case back to the Appeal Court for a decision. This looked very promising: information about guests at a seminar in 2006 looked much more like archive material than journalism. However, in fact the Court of Appeal subsequently ruled against Sugar, and a further appeal was made to the Supreme Court. A final resolution to the case is expected at the start of 2012. Until then the details of the climate change seminar remain under wraps.

At around the same time I received the latest of a series of emails from Harrabin himself. These emails had begun in the wake of Climategate, when I had gained a relatively significant media profile after the publication of my book *The Hockey Stick Illusion* and also my exposure of the failures of the Climategate inquiries. At irregular intervals throughout 2010, Harrabin had emailed asking me to comment on various developments in the news. At the same time, many in the sceptic community had begun to notice a change in the tone of Harrabin's reporting, with much less greenery and much more journalistic inquiry on view. In particular, Harrabin had picked up on my blog posts about the issues with the integrity of the Climategate inquiries, and had filed several probing reports – indeed he was one of the only journalists to do so. What caused this shift is not clear, but it is possible that our discovery of CMEP's activities may have induced a more cautious approach to sceptics.

Having received a several emails from Harrabin over the previous months, I was not especially surprised to get another at the end of June, but the title suggested this message was different: 'FOI appeal - Montford v ICO & BBC'.

The email was a forwarded copy of a message the BBC's barrister had written to Harrabin, asking for copies of the emails I had requested. Amazingly, this email appeared to be the first time that Harrabin had heard of the FOI request I had issued some two years earlier, as he explained in his covering note:

Andrew I have just picked up this request. Ring me and I will tell you what you want to know. FOI is not the right course here. Roger.

Unfortunately, when we spoke Harrabin would only tell me what I wanted to know on condition that I did not reveal what he said. The details of our conversation must therefore remain confidential.

Brian Cox at the Royal Television Society

By the end of the summer of 2010 our submission to the Jones inquiry was ready to go. It covered the full story of CMEP, the climate change seminar, as well as our own views on the BBC's climate change coverage. From where we stood, we felt that our revelations could leave Jones in little doubt that there were some serious questions to be answered and we were certain that he would have to investigate what we were saying. At the end of October I emailed the submission off, receiving a polite note of thanks from Jones himself. He would, he said, certainly take our views into account.

A long silence followed, broken only by an intervention from an unexpected quarter. In December 2010, the physicist Brian Cox gave a lecture to the Royal Television Society entitled 'Science – a challenge to TV Orthodoxy'. Much of the lecture discussed TV coverage of climate change, addressing in particular *The Great Global Warming Swindle* (see above), which Cox described as 'total bollocks', and also *Climate Wars*, the three part series that the BBC had produced in response. Cox felt the latter was the epitome of good science broadcasting.

Listening to Cox talk, it appeared for a time as if he might stand up for the right of dissenters to speak freely and make the point that the BBC had a duty to allow them to be heard. Indeed at one point he quoted John Stuart Mill approvingly:

We can never be sure that the opinion we are endeavoring to stifle is a false opinion; and even if we were sure, stifling it would be an evil still.

However, he then went on to make the extraordinary claim that where a dissenting opinion conflicted with the scientific mainstream, it should be flagged as being a 'polemic' rather than a documentary – a suggestion that appeared to be tantamount to flagging it to viewers as 'wrong'. Who would make the assessment of which programmes were 'polemic' and which were documentaries was left unclear. Cox appeared somewhat concerned at what he was suggesting, wondering if what he was proposing was in fact 'authoritarian' or even 'Orwellian'. Nevertheless that is where he left it. Newbery and I compared notes afterwards, and agreed that it might well be a signal of what we could expect from the Jones report.

The Jones report

The Jones report was finally issued on 20 July 2010 and it was everything we had feared it would be. Jones' treatment of our submission was, to put it politely, quite shameful and it is hard to think of any excuse for what he decided to write about our evidence, which grossly misrepresented our concerns.

> A submission made to this Review by Andrew Montford and Tony Newbery (both active in the anti-global-warming movement, and the former the author of *The Hockey Stick Illusion: Climategate and the Corruption of Science*) devotes much of its content to criticising not the data on temperatures but the membership of a BBC seminar on the topic in 2006, and to a lengthy discussion

as to whether its Environment Analyst was carrying out BBC duties or acting as a freelance during an environment programme at Cambridge University. The factual argument, even for activists, appears to be largely over but parts of the BBC are taking a long time to notice.

Why we would have submitted evidence about temperature data to a review on BBC editorial policy is anybody's guess, but Jones' wording suggests firstly that he had barely looked at what we had written and secondly that he chose to issue what amounted to an insult rather than deal with our submission with integrity.

Jones' recommendations, meanwhile, appeared to be completely in line with what Cox had suggested:

> I recommend that the BBC takes a less rigid view of 'due impartiality' as it applies to science (in practice and not just in its guidelines) and takes into account the non-contentious nature of some material and the need to avoid giving undue attention to marginal opinion.

In addition, and apparently in order to add further insult to injury, Jones had decided to try to malign one of the UK's most prominent sceptics, Nigel Lawson:

> The impression of active debate is promoted by prominent individuals such as Lord Monckton and Lord Lawson. The BBC still gives space to them to make statements that are not supported by the facts; that (in a February 2011 *The Daily Politics* show) 95% of the carbon dioxide in the atmosphere comes from natural sources, while in fact human activity has been responsible for a 40% rise in concentration, or (a November 2009

Today programme) that volcanoes produce more of the gas than do humans (the balance is a hundred times in the opposite direction).

The impression given was clearly that Lawson and Monckton had been guilty of saying these things, but Jones soon found himself threatened with libel by Lawson, who noted that he had never said anything of the sort. Jones had no choice but to issue a correction and apology. Nevertheless, it looked as though it was game set and match to the Cambridge Media and Environment Programme.

Earth Reports

Soon, however, the tide was to change emphatically. On 15 November 2011 a series of events was triggered that may finally have led to the exposing of CMEP. The cue for this dramatic change was a report by the BBC Trust into a series of programmes that had been purchased from programme makers outside the BBC for zero or minimal cost. A freelance journalist had discovered that the BBC had, in effect, been accepting illicit sponsorship for current affairs programmes from a variety of green activist bodies. He had reported what he had found to the BBC Trust, who had been forced to launch an inquiry. After a long investigation, the allegations proved to be completely correct and the scandal soon hit the newspapers. One example of what had been uncovered was given by the *Independent*:

> One of the programmes in breach of guidelines was 'Taking the Credit' made for BBC World on the subject of Africa and climate change by the award-winning British production company Rockhopper Television. The Trust found that the programme had effectively been sponsored by the Envirotrade organisation, despite the fact that

current affairs programmes are prohibited from using sponsorship. Envirotrade was featured in a positive light in the programme but 'viewers were unaware that there was a funding arrangement in place,' said the Trust report.

The Trust's report had made clear that these programmes were being handed over to the BBC for a price that was often close to nil. In essence then, environmentalists had been given slots on BBC's overseas channels to advance their propaganda. It was an extraordinary state of affairs.

When I relayed the story to my blog readers I embedded a video of one of the shows involved – *Earth Reporters*, a series about environmental issues around the world – so that people could see just how naked a propaganda piece it was. At first I just viewed enough of the video to assess it for myself, but the following day I decided to take a another look. The programme was just as bad as I had first thought, and I struggled to watch it through, but I managed to hold on until the end, which was just as well. As the closing credits rolled, a name suddenly caught my eye: credited as academic adviser to the programme was none other than Joe Smith of CMEP. It was a quite extraordinary find: the man who had run the seminar that had concluded that sceptics should be kept off the airwaves had also been involved in a propaganda series broadcast by the BBC on behalf of environmentalists. I posted a blog article about it soon afterwards.

The news that I had discovered the CMEP connection spread quickly, and shortly afterwards I discovered that Smith had put up a response to my posting on his own blog, the existence of which I had hitherto been unaware. Although his post was long, in essence it told us little that we didn't know already. He discussed CMEP, noting that its work had ended in 2009 at around the time Tony Newbery had first questioned him about his work with Harrabin. He mentioned his work on *Earth Reporters* and said that he had been very happy with this series. He argued that the problem from the BBC Trust's perspective was with the fact that the 'sponsorship' had not been disclosed, and suggested that the content of the programmes was not being criticised. In essence we were little further forward.

Over the following days, more information trickled out about the BBC's involvement with environmentalists and also some more interesting connections to the CMEP story. For example, one of the programme-makers involved in the scandal, a company called TVE, was involved with the IBT, the organisation that had also been involved in the CMEP seminars. We also discovered an interview with Sir David Attenborough, in which he discussed his involvement with the *Earth Reporters* series. More importantly, he revealed other sources of sponsorship:

> The series has been made possible by the generosity of WWF and the MacArthur Foundation, which have provided more than half the $900,000 it is costing to provide a regular service. Other finance has come from such sources as the Global Environment Facility, the World Health Organization, UNEP, and the Secretariat of the Ramsar Convention.

The involvement of WWF was particularly interesting because Newbery and I had noted, in Joe Smith's *Risk Analysis* paper, the disclosure that some of the CMEP seminars had been funded by WWF as well. It was hard to come away with a favourable impression of the BBC's independence and impartiality.

By the following weekend, the story was gathering legs, with both the *Sunday Telegraph* and the *Mail on Sunday* giving extensive coverage to what I had found. When I had discussed my latest findings on the blog, several commenters had expressed disquiet over the fact that CMEP had received funding from the Tyndall Centre because the centre is so closely aligned with the Climatic Research Unit of Climategate fame – both are sited on the same campus of the University of East Anglia. This angle to the story had been picked up by the Mail, who accused Harrabin of having had a conflict of interest when he reported on the Climategate affair the previous year.

Meanwhile, Smith had responded to the Sunday Telegraph's article, defending himself of the accusation of being a green activist:

> Christopher Booker describes me as a 'climate activist'. In the interests of accuracy and fairness I want to state clearly here that that is a label which I flatly reject. The research and policy dimensions of climate change are not simple or easy. Myself and thousands of scholars around the world will need to be thoughtful, open minded and dogged in doing justice to their complexity. People need to keep in touch and exchange views in a thoughtful and civil way. I would have welcomed a conversation with Christopher as he prepared his piece but was not given the opportunity. The free exchange of views about demanding topics is one of the things that the seminars that his piece refers to have been all about.

This was a remarkable stand to take given what we knew about Smith's activities and his writings. Shortly afterwards, I posted a video of a lecture he had given in 2009, which made his defence seem still more preposterous. As he noted to his audience at the time:

> In much of my work I have combined thinking and writing about these issues with direct engagement. Hence I draw on the term 'action

research' to describe projects that generate research but are simultaneously designed to make a difference to the way the world is.

Climategate 2.0

Despite the excitement over these new revelations, there appeared to be little else to say, and Newbery and I appeared to have reached the end of the story. I cast around for some other aspect of the CMEP affair to write about and on 21 November, I posted a short piece about the funding Smith and Harrabin had received from the Tyndall Centre, noting that payment of the invoices had been authorised by Professor Mike Hulme. To many of my blog readers, this was a familiar name, since Hulme had appeared regularly in the Climategate emails released in 2009, although he had not been seen as having a central role. His involvement in the CMEP seminars was a minor point of interest, answering the need for material on the blog for a few more hours, but was little more than that.

However, the next day – 22 November 2011 – everything changed once again, when a second tranche of Climategate emails was released onto the web. The first batch, released two years earlier, had focused narrowly on scientific issues and on the activities of two members of the CRU's staff – Phil Jones and Keith Briffa. However, in this second release, many more of the messages involved Hulme, who had at one time been a member of CRU staff. There were also several emails that touched on media issues and many that were damning of the BBC. One notable example was the one in which Alex Kirby, an environment correspondent, had mocked the idea of the BBC being a neutral in the climate debate, referring to 'the objective impartial (ho ho) BBC that we are'. More dramatically, a number of the new emails spoke directly to the question of CMEP's activities. Here, finally, after nearly five years of research, was proof that the BBC's independence and impartiality had been subverted by a combination of activist journalism, activist scientists and environmentalists.

Email 0306, dating back to 2004, was particularly important. This involved correspondence between the Tyndall Centre's PR man, Asher Minns, and Joe Smith. Minns was inviting Smith to speak at the Tyndall Assembly, a meeting of Tyndall staff and their wider network of colleagues. Speakers at the assembly were to include Rajendra Pachauri, the head of the IPCC, and Jim Skea, the director of a UK energy research centre, so it is clear that this was an important occasion. Minns began his message by explaining what he thought Smith should cover in his talk, and suggested that a suitable topic would be the CMEP seminars:

> My thinking for your part is that you give an overview of your BBC-Cambridge series and its objectives and outcomes and challenges. I would also quite like to hear what you see as the challenges in the relationship between the media and climate change research, and the role you see Tyndall playing. These are just my ideas for now – we can chat on Tuesday.

Smith replied, copying Hulme. The first thing on his mind appeared to be money to support the ongoing activities of CMEP:

> ... first wanted to test the ground about whether Tyndall is in a position to support the seminar programme next year (am approaching 3/4 of the current club of sponsors now so that we've got time to make other arrangements if need be.) The only change I anticipate is that we won't be

asking WWF to support the seminars: Roger particularly feels the association could be compromising to the 'neutral' reputation should anyone look at it closely. We'll be asking [British Gas] to make up the difference and would continue to ask Tyndall and DEFRA for £5K p.a.

Here again was recognition that CMEP had been funded by environmentalists, but also the revelation that Smith and Harrabin were fully aware that this situation was untenable for the BBC, which claimed to be impartial.

Smith then moved on to discuss CMEP's future plans.

Our target next year is to get complex long term sustainability issues under the net of Westminster election coverage before the next election with a residential seminar in Feb and something at White City for output level people closer to the election. Already got some [senior] people within BBC excited [about] the residential [seminar]. But your thoughts [are] welcome about other specific things we should pick off.

Next he discussed plans for the speech to the Tyndall people, and here CMEP's activities began to look highly problematic (emphasis added):

Second: query [about] how I should [be] using my slot at the Assembly:

I imagine that the ten mins might split into the following: a summary of the seminar [programme] Tyndall has supported: its aims, method and impact (inc my view of its failings...), with specific [reference] to climate change (6 mins) outline of future work (*getting global environmental change and sustainability issues into mainstream stories 'by stealth'*) (2 mins) Needs the CME programme doesn't meet? Media awareness for specialists; issues awareness for early career media people (1 minute) Provocation about the role of climate change research and policy community in delivering improved coverage (2 mins) Is that the sort of thing you had in mind?

The idea of getting green angles into mainstream news stories 'by stealth' looked like a highly questionable course of action for a reputable broadcaster, looking more like campaigning than reporting the news. And if this wasn't interesting enough, Smith's third topic of conversation was a plan for a research project that would inform decision-makers in the media and in policy circles (in the quote, Jacquie may well be Jacquie Burgess, another UEA academic):

> Third to outline thoughts on research project I mentioned to you:
>
> Things have moved on quite quickly in the wake of a series of conversations in the last few days. In the same week as the Tyndall workshop I was at meetings on sustainable consumption and development issues in media. All of these helped to form in my mind an extended piece of work requiring a well designed team effort.
>
> There's an urgent need to explore... source–media–audience relationship in the round (Jacquie's 'circuit of culture') on a number of issues: climate change; biodiversity loss; poverty; [pollution] risk, in a major project with a bundle of partners over a period of e.g. three years (though it would at the same time develop a body of material that could represent a qualitative time series that could be worked with over the longer term). Its very important in my view

that this is research feeds directly back into decision-[maker] conversations (policy and above all media). I hope and think that the seminars have laid the ground for this within [the] BBC, and would design the research to work closely with the design of the seminars (though I'll continue to construct a Chinese wall between the two).

Finally, Smith explained the reaction of senior BBC decision-makers to his ideas.

There is senior BBC buy in for the approach I want to pursue on both News and TV side, and I'm confident after some informal conversations [government departments] and NGOs would also want to play. I'd really like to work with Jacquie on it and have emailed her about that [yesterday].

Would be good to talk to you and/or [Hulme] on the research project - I appreciate that as [Open University] based I'm not in a position to bid for Tyndall funds etc, but in my mind it would be important to have the network involved in any case, and although I've not needed to source major research funding before ('pen, paper and train ticket please') I think there are resources out there for this kind of work. The publics/group work that I'd like to get Jacquie interested in would be resource intensive and ideally I want to either buy myself out (ideal if [Open University] politics allow) or get research [associate] on board to work with the 'source communities' and media lot.

Email 0306 was bad enough, but there was more in some of the other emails. For example, there was the one in which

Mike Hulme appeared to give away the CMEP's raison d'etre (emphasis added):

> Did anyone hear Stott vs. Houghton on *Today*, Radio 4 this morning? Woeful stuff really. This is one reason why Tyndall is sponsoring the Cambridge Media/Environment Programme to starve this type of reporting at source.

In another message, CRU's director Phil Jones seemed to confirm that BBC output had become just what Hulme had hoped:

> The reporting of climate stories within the media (especially the BBC) is generally one-sided, i.e. the counter argument is rarely made.

Shortly after the Climategate 2 emails had been released, a reader of my blog had noticed that Roger Harrabin had at one time been a member of the advisory board of the Tyndall Centre, and soon afterwards, I noticed another email that mentioned Harrabin. This had previously been overlooked because his name had been misspelt, but it was clear from the context that it could be no-one else. The email was sent from a senior scientist called John Shepherd and discussed the idea of setting up a website where sceptic claims about the climate could be countered. The emphasis is added.

> Many thanks for your very helpful comments. Essentially I agree on all counts, and indeed the 'sceptics ask, scientists answer' web-page that you have set up is exactly the sort of thing I had in mind as a possible minimal response that we (Tyndall et al, and even maybe the Royal Society if it wants to get involved) might undertake. Wherever possible this could/should refer to other reputable sites (incl IPCC, Hadley Centre, the ones you mention, etc etc) rather

than duplicating the material. I would envisage that such a site could be maintained by a consortium of the willing, in this case involving (say) Tyndall, Hadley & PIK. We could then asked the [Royal Society] (et al) to mention it and link to it on some sort of 'sound science' page on their own web-site(s) (Rachel, do you think that this might fly ?).

We had an interesting debate on this at the Tyndall Advisory Board last week, and *the consensus was very much in line with your views, except for the journalist present (Roger Horobin), who wanted something more pro-active.* I am more sympathetic to his view than most of you, I think, but the question is what more would be useful, effective, and not too burdensome? So far I don't think I have identified anything, but I do think that the sort of web-page mentioned above would be a start, and so I am copying this to Asher Minns, for him to consider and discuss with John & Mike at Tyndall Central.

The commissioner and the tribunal

The media paid little attention to the second batch of Climategate emails. However, one of the articles that did appear picked up on the the BBC's involvement. In an article in the *Mail on Sunday*, journalist David Rose highlighted the links between CMEP, the BBC and the University of East Anglia, focusing particularly on the scandal-ridden university's funding of Harrabin's seminars. But even coverage in such a widely read newspaper was not enough to gain momentum for the story, and media attention soon shifted elsewhere.

With the publicity surrounding the CMEP story having made so little lasting impact, our hopes were now pinned on a successful outcome to our FOI requests to the BBC, which would enable us to confirm that the seminar attendees were as Richard North had described them. Our hopes, however, were increasingly forlorn. The Information Commissioner had already thrown out our appeals, and we knew that it would therefore be a long and arduous process to get his decision overturned. This would involve an appeal to the Information Tribunal, a step that we could not take lightly. While appeals to the commissioner are relatively informal, usually involving nothing more onerous than an exchange of letters, the Tribunal is a formal process overseen by a panel of judges, and cases are often argued by barristers. Perhaps more importantly for us, it is at least theoretically possible for costs to be awarded against unsuccessful litigants. However, after due consideration, we decided to take the plunge.

It was clear that the precedent set by Supreme Court's decision in the Sugar case was going to go a long way towards determining the scope of the BBC's journalism exemption and it was therefore was going to be critical to the decision taken in our own cases. We therefore decided to apply for a stay of the case pending a clarification of the law in the higher courts. Our wait was to be a long one. Sugar was nothing if not a very determined man, taking his case right through the appeals process, almost to its conclusion. Only his untimely death at the start of 2011 seemed to spell the end of his campaign. Or so we thought. Remarkably, however, Sugar's widow was given leave to continue the case he had begun and so, it seemed, we would have a final answer after all.

The decision, when it came, was a disappointment. Although the scope of the BBC's derogation was narrowed somewhat there was a lot less movement than I would have liked. But while I was downcast, Newbery would not be beaten, arguing that there was still scope within the decision for us to make a case at the Tribunal. We resolved to continue with our appeals.

My own case, revised in the light of the Sugar decision, was that Harrabin's email correspondence with Smith should be disclosed. I made my case on two main grounds: firstly that correspondence dealing with arrangements for the seminar was so far removed from 'journalistic purposes' as to rule out the application of the exemption, and secondly that the nature of the attendees, as evidenced by North's observations, was such that the seminar could not reasonably be construed as bona fide journalism anyway. If these two strands to my case failed, I suggested, the Tribunal should also address the question of whether the information should be disclosed under the Environmental Information Regulations. With the revised case lodged, we quickly moved towards a decision.

The Tribunal's ruling arrived in the middle of August 2012 and was laid out in a very strange way. My grounds of appeal had been set out in an intended order of application – that the seminar was not bona fide journalism and failing this that the correspondence I sought was far removed from journalism. If all else failed I asked the court to then consider if the Environmental Information Regulations should apply. The court, however, noted that it was *not* going to address the arguments as I had put them:

> ... it may assist the Appellant and others who may read this decision if the EIR points are addressed first before turning to the Derogation issues.

Several pages of legal analysis followed, focused entirely on my fallback arguments about EIR. Remarkably, the response to my primary and secondary arguments was in essence restricted to a single sentence:

> Focusing finally on the answer to the question... does the Derogation apply? – the Tribunal finds that it does.

This was supported by a summary of the Supreme Court decision on the Sugar case, none of which had anything to do with my primary argument that the seminar was not bona fide journalism. Likewise, my second argument about the directness of purpose was completely ignored. This was very strange to say the least.

Meanwhile, Newbery's appeal – for the names of the attendees at the seminar, together with the agenda and minutes and other records relating it – was proceeding in parallel, but at a somewhat slower pace. There was one crucial difference between our two cases though. Unlike me, Newbery had opted for a hearing in person rather than by exchange of letters and he therefore had the delectable prospect of being able to cross-examine the BBC's head of news, Helen Boaden.

The hearing took place over two days at the end of October 2012. In the London basement in which the hearing was held there was a panel of three judges – one professional lawyer and two lay members – and opposite them the parties involved in the case. The Information Commissioner was represented by a barrister, but the BBC had arrived in quite extraordinary force. As proceedings opened their party numbered no fewer than eleven people, of whom two were witnesses. The corporation was paying for no fewer than six lawyers, two of whom were barristers. Newbery, meanwhile, was accompanied by his wife.

So before a word had been uttered it was clear that there was to be no equality of arms. But Newbery was soon to discover that this was not the least of his problems. As a contemporary report explained:

> When it came to a cross examination by Newbery, David Marks QC, the presiding tribunal judge, threw a thick protective cloak around the BBC's star witness, refusing to allow the blogger to pose

many of his questions to Boaden directly. As a result, most remained answered.

The application of the Chatham House rule was a key part of the BBC's defence, with Boaden arguing that the rule prevented disclosure of lists of attendees. Her claim clearly contradicted the popular understanding of the rule as well as the Chatham House web page Newbery and I seen years earlier (see above). However, Newbery had found to his surprise that Boaden was citing a different version of the Chatham House web page:

Q. Can a list of attendees at the meeting be published?
A. No - the list of attendees should not be circulated beyond those participating in the meeting.

Apparently, some time after we had originally seen it, Chatham House had issued new advice on the meaning of the rule. However, since this change clearly post-dated the seminar it was hard to see how the BBC could rely on it to protect the identities of its experts. Moreover, Newbery noted that subsequent to Boaden preparing her submission to the Tribunal, the Chatham House website had changed *again*, reverting back to the original formulation about considering the spirit of the rule. This rather took the ground out from underneath Boaden's feet, but it remained to be seen how the judge would view these arguments, or indeed the rather suspect suggestion that the Chatham House rule allowed public bodies to trump the Freedom of Information Act.

Apart from rebutting Boaden's arguments about the Chatham House rule, Newbery's case rested on the idea that information peripheral to the seminar, such as invitations and the agenda, was not held for the purposes of journalism but for archival purposes. He argued that in view of the Supreme

Court's ruling, the information he wanted would have to be disclosed. However, the presiding judge seemed not to understand Newbery's case and brushed it aside.

Despite this, some useful information did emerge from the hearing. Not the least was Boaden's apparent acceptance that the BBC Trust's claim that the seminar attendees were scientists was false. As she explained in her written statement to the Tribunal the attendees were:

> ...representatives from business, campaigners, NGOS, communications experts, people from the 'front line', scientists with contrasting views and academics.

So at last Newbery had confirmed what Richard North had told us so long before. There was one other interesting bit of information too. In her introductory comments, Boaden noted the names of the managers who had authorised the setting up of the seminar series:

> [The seminar] was organised by an ad hoc partnership known as the Cambridge Media and Environmental Programme ('CMEP') in conjunction with the BBC News senior management team, at first overseen by Tony Hall [the then director of BBC News].

Hall's involvement in authorising the setting up the seminar scheme had been alluded to somewhat vaguely in an interview Harrabin had given right back in 2007, but this was our first confirmation that the seminar series had the full blessing of senior management. However, these two snippets of information were minor victories in a case that looked very much as if it was heading rapidly towards an unfavourable conclusion.

The Tribunal's decision was apparently in record time. Normally, decisions are published four to six weeks after a hearing, but for Newbery's case the panel felt able to to move much, much more quickly. The BBC, they announced just ten days after proceedings in London had closed, could keep the details of the seminar and its mysterious attendees a secret.

Hue and cry

Although Newbery had only his wife to support him as he battled with the judges and the serried ranks of the BBC's legal team, he had one other sympathiser. Andrew Orlowski, a journalist with tech-magazine *The Register* attended the first day of the hearing to observe Newbery's cross-examination of Boaden. Shortly afterwards he posted the first of a series of articles discussing the seminar and, more importantly, the Information Tribunal hearing.

Orlowski had been disturbed by the behaviour of the panel of judges and had done some digging to find out if there was anything in their backgrounds that might explain it. What he found was highly alarming. Alison Lowton, one of the lay panel members, was a former solicitor at the London Borough of Camden where she had been director of legal services. This was unremarkable, but as Orlowski observed, some research suggested that she had been on the wrong end of an FOI request herself and consequently might not be a big fan of transparency legislation:

> The former director of legal services of Camden Council took a six-figure severance package in 2007 when her post was abolished. Camden fought to keep the details of the settlement away from freedom-of-information requests.

Remarkably, however, the other lay judge was even more surprising. As Orlowski observed, just a few months earlier, former Haringey councillor Narendra Makanji had demonstrated his antipathy to global warming sceptics on his Twitter account, referring to them by the offensive term 'deniers' and encouraging others to do so too:

> Michael Hintze who dines at No 10 is backer of Global Warming Policy Foundation, climate change deniers fronted by Nigel Lawson. [Please retweet].

Orlowski's revelations were extraordinary, but did seem to explain the judge's behaviour. Newbery and I were staggered.

At the time of the ruling in my own hearing I had not even glanced at the names of the judges, but in the light of what had happened to Newbery the way my case had been brushed aside was now ringing all sorts of alarm bells. And when I checked the Tribunal ruling it was just as I suspected: Alison Lowton had also been a lay member on my own panel too. The other lay member was called Rosalind Tatam who, according to her biography on the Tribunal website, was a 'representative on Chelmsford Diocesan Synod and its Environment Group'; she is also the former company secretary of something called Christian Ecology Link.

It didn't look good.

28gate

Orlowski is an experienced journalist and his article in the Register conjured up a compelling picture of the lone pensioner doing battle with the might of the BBC and an unsympathetic panel of judges. Newbery may not have won, but the outrage engendered by Orlowski's article was to prove the BBC's undoing regardless. News of what had happened at the Tribunal quickly spread; first to the blogs and then to the mainstream media, a rare development for a tribunal case. It will no doubt have been a shock to the judges to find their obscure corner of the legal system being discussed in the pages of the *Sunday Telegraph*. All this attention focused on our long hunt for the truth had the inevitable result that the attention of the blogosphere started to focus on the seminar. Before long, new lines of inquiry started to appear.

Maurizio Morabito is an Italian-born IT consultant and occasional blogger. Now based in London, he is well known on the climate blogs where he is a regular commenter. Outraged by what he read of Newbery's treatment, Morabito started to see if he could uncover details of the seminar anywhere on the internet. Following the trail we had uncovered all those years earlier, he found himself on the IBT website. Newbery and I and others had scoured these pages for details of the seminar, but the only document we had found had no details of the attendees. We had gone further and scoured the Wayback Machine – an archive of old webpages – for details too, but had found nothing.

Morabito, however, struck gold. Noticing a dead hyperlink on the IBT website he decided to look up the missing page in the Wayback Machine and there it was: the list of names (see Tables 1 and 2). Five years on, we had it.

The names were just as Richard North had said – the 'we must support Kyoto' school of climate change activists. Greenpeace, Stop Climate Chaos, Oneworld.net, the International Institute for Environment and Development, the list went on and on. There were, as Boaden had indicated, business people too but even most of these were green businessmen. Andrew Dlugolecki, billed as an insurance consultant, turned out to be an ex-insurance industry consultant who was actually working at the University of East Anglia and regularly campaigned on global warming. The representative of BP came from their CO2 Project and NPower's man came from their renewables arm.

There were other intriguing names too: a representative of TVE, one of the companies involved in the free programming scandal and a representative of the US embassy. But what was clear above all was that there were virtually no scientists in attendance. Only Mike Hulme and one other attendee could have been said to have expertise in the area of climate change and even the representative of the Scott Polar Research Institute turned out to be a historian rather than a scientist. The truth was out. The BBC Trust had misled the public.

Fallout

As we watched the fallout from the exposure of the names, more disturbing facts began to emerge. Further examination of the Wayback Machine revealed that it was not only the list of names that had been removed from the IBT's version of events – someone had also taken steps to cover up the effect of the seminars. The webpage had originally explained in frank terms what was going on:

> The International Broadcasting Trust (IBT) has been lobbying the BBC, on behalf of all the major UK aid and development agencies, to improve its coverage of the developing world. One of the aims is to take this coverage out of the box of news and current affairs, so that the lives of people in the rest of the world, and the issues which affect them, become a regular feature of a much wider range of BBC programmes, for example dramas and features... [The seminars] have had a significant impact on the BBC's output.

In the new version, however, this had been replaced with a bland statement, with no mention of lobbying, explaining that the seminars were about exploring 'how we can more effectively represent our interconnected world'.

The timings of these changes were interesting too. The IBT's original report on the seminar, with the list of names intact, dated back to the middle of 2007. However, the revised version without the list of names, which Newbery and I had seen all those years earlier, appears to have been prepared in the middle of 2008 at around the same time the details of Matt Prescott's meeting with Harrabin had disappeared from the web. It looked as though the attempts to obscure the details of the seminars had been more thorough than we thought.

Conclusions

The BBC's journalists and management have been using the corporation's vast resources to promote the views of green pressure groups; that much seems clear. That the corporation should allow itself to be influenced by a group of green activists is bad enough. That it should wheel out senior executives to hear the message of special interest groups is appalling, but perhaps not unexpected given Joe Smith's observation that there was senior BBC management buy-in to the idea of the seminar programme. That buy-in seems unequivocally to have delivered the change that the seminar attendees wanted, with Boaden noting in her evidence to the Information Tribunal a range of programmes that had been produced as a result of the seminar. But as she also explained to the Tribunal, the purpose of the seminar was not really about programme ideas but about changing the corporation's whole approach to environmental issues. It was not just news and current affairs programmes that were affected either. The range of BBC executives in attendance suggests strongly that the seminar was intended to inform every aspect of the BBC's output and that the intention was not only to sideline sceptics in news programmes, but also science, weather, features, special events and education and even comedy, entertainment and drama. Examination of BBC output since 2006 suggests that everything the seminar set out to achieve was realised over the following years.

The revelation that the BBC has allowed itself to be subverted by outside interests is bad enough, but its determination to conduct its affairs in secret has been just as damaging – it is a commonplace observation that the cover-up is worse than the crime. This refusal to reveal the details of how such an important aspect of BBC policy was formulated is all the more extraordinary when one reads the BBC Trust's view on openness. In the very same report which had attracted our attention to the seminar in the first place – *From Seesaw to Wagonwheel* – author John Bridcut had made a bold declaration about how the corporation would retain public trust:

> If the trust is to be earned, impartiality can no longer be served out from on high, along with dollops of nectar and ambrosia: it has to be shared with and understood by our increasingly active audience.

Large chunks of the report were devoted to this same theme, and it seems clear that if the BBC had heeded Bridcut's advice, the damage caused by 28gate might have been avoided. As it was put in the report:

> It is true that impartiality always used to be discussed behind closed doors at Broadcasting House and Television Centre...The reality is that you can't close the doors any more...the information will leak out sooner or later, and the BBC will end up looking defensive or worse. But if it keeps the doors open, it will help the audience to understand how impartiality works, and trust will grow...Every now and then, openness entails a risk of unfavourable publicity – but that is a daily part of the heat in the BBC kitchen. The greater prize is the maintenance of the audience's trust. That trust is the BBC 's most precious resource.

The CMEP affair shows unequivocally that the BBC is on a very different path.

The story of the seminar and the BBC's attempts to hide what had happened cannot have come at a worse time for the corporation. The names emerged in the immediate wake of the Savile affair – the revelation that BBC management had covered up the activities of a paedophile in their midst – and the McAlpine affair – in which over-eager journalists had attempted to accuse a senior Conservative politician of paedophilia. In fact, Boaden was attending the Information Tribunal just as the crisis was breaking and she was most needed at her desk. The decision by management to cover up the Trust's misrepresentation of the seminar attendees has appalled those who have read about it in the media. Spending hundreds of thousands of pounds in legal fees in repulsing the simple and reasonable FOI requests of a pair of bloggers suggests a willingness to put personal and corporate interests first and represents a wilful neglect of BBC management's role as stewards of public funds. There was precisely *no* public interest in keeping the identity of the seminar attendees a secret – as we now know the names of seminar attendees had been routinely published on the IBT website. The objective of removing the names from that website and the expensive attempts to fend off inquiries was simply to protect BBC insiders from the scandal that threatened them, and seems to have been done with few, if any, concerns about being called to account. This fact should worry those who pay the licence fee.

The secrecy that the BBC enforces over all of its activities is like a throwback to the Cold War. In recent years government has increasingly opened its activities to public scrutiny through the introduction of transparency legislation, bringing numerous benefits in terms of accountability and exposure of corruption and graft. But as these welcome developments have started to change the culture of the state, the BBC has battened down the hatches, exploiting its hard-won derogation from the FOI Act to its limit. In the new climate of openness, the BBC's enthusiasm for operating beyond public scrutiny and doing deals behind closed doors is an aberration. That the corporation needs to keep its journalistic sources secret is accepted on all sides. That it feels it must keep secret the identities of the 'experts' it has consulted on an issue of vital public importance is much harder to rationalise unless one accepts Joe Smith's observation that there was buy-in by top management to the seminar programme. If management knew and approved of the corporation's output – all of it – being adapted to the demands of green lobbyists then we must conclude that the secrecy adopted was simply a way of ensuring that the subversion of the national broadcaster had the full blessing of those in control.

The role of the BBC Trust – the body charged with representing the public interest – in these events is less clear than that of management, but there are few indications that the public interest was foremost in the minds of those involved. It is hard to ascertain if the misrepresentation of the nature of the seminar in the *Seesaw to Wagonwheel* report was deliberate or if the Trust was misled. In the wake of the media furore over the revelation of the 28 attendees' identities, the report's author, ex-BBC producer John Bridcut, has said that he has no recollection of who had told him that they had been scientists. However, there still is much that should worry licence-fee payers. When Newbery informed the Trust of our concerns about the seminar he was systematically blocked by its staff, who ensured that no word of the affair reached those who needed to know. This is hardly the act of a body that is working on behalf of the public. The report that the Trust commissioned from Professor Steve Jones was little better. Jones was paid tens of thousands of pounds for his work on the BBC's inquiry into impartiality in its science coverage. In return he treated the submission of evidence from me and Tony Newbery with contempt and an almost complete lack of professional integrity. In the wake of his report, he has been made to look extraordinarily foolish by the publication of the BBC Trust's report into illicit sponsorship by green groups and, above all, by the revelations of the Climategate emails, which demonstrated clearly and unequivocally that our concerns were entirely correct. Yet even this was not enough for the Trust, who did not lift a finger in response.

Amazingly, with the story of the seminars all over the newspapers yet again after the list of names was published, the Trust has *still* maintained its silence. Its only relevant action has been to appoint Tony Hall (now Lord Hall), the man who had authorised the setting up of the seminar series, as the new director-general.

There can only be one explanation. The BBC is rotten and the Trust knows it. They know that we know it and they know that we know that they know. Their only hope of salvation lies in a stubborn refusal to acknowledge those they are paid to represent.

Table 1: The seminar attendees: the 'specialists'

Robert May	Oxford University and Imperial College London
Mike Hulme	Tyndall Centre, UEA
Blake Lee-Harwood	Greenpeace
Dorthe Dahl-Jensen	Niels Bohr Institute
Michael Bravo	Scott Polar Research Institute
Andrew Dlugolecki	Insurance industry consultant
Trevor Evans	US Embassy
Colin Challen MP	Chair, All Party Group on Climate Change
Anuradha Vittachi	Oneworld.net
Andrew Simms	New Economics Foundation
Claire Foster	Church of England
Saleemul Huq	IIED
Poshendra Satyal Pravat	Open University
Li Moxuan	Climate campaigner, Greenpeace
Tadesse Dadi	Tearfund Ethiopia
Iain Wright	CO2 Project Manager, BP
Ashok Sinha	Stop Climate Chaos
Andy Atkins	Advocacy Director, Tearfund
Matthew Farrow	CBI
Rafael Hidalgo	TV/multimedia producer
Cheryl Campbell	Television for the Environment
Kevin McCullough	Npower Renewables
Richard D North	Institute of Economic Affairs
Steve Widdicombe	Plymouth Marine Labs
Joe Smith	The Open University
Mark Galloway	Director, IBT
Anita Neville	E3G
Eleni Andreadis	Harvard University
Jos Wheatley	Global Environment Assets Team, DFID
Tessa Tennant	Chair, AsRia

Table 2: The seminar attendees: the BBC

Jana Bennett	Director of Television
Sacha Baveystock	Executive Producer, Science
Helen Boaden	Director of News
Andrew Lane	Manager, Weather, TV News
Anne Gilchrist	Executive Editor Indies & Events, CBBC
Dominic Vallely	Executive Editor, Entertainment
Eleanor Moran	Development Executive, Drama
Elizabeth McKay	Project Executive, Education
Emma Swain	Commissioning Editor, Specialist Factual
Fergal Keane	(Chair), Foreign Affairs Correspondent
Fran Unsworth	Head of Newsgathering
George Entwistle	Head of TV Current Affairs
Glenwyn Benson	Controller, Factual TV
John Lynch	Creative Director, Specialist Factual
Jon Plowman	Head of Comedy
Jon Williams	TV Editor Newsgathering
Karen O'Connor	Editor, This World, Current Affairs
Catriona McKenzie	Tightrope Pictures
Liz Molyneux	Editorial Executive, Factual
Matt Morris	Head of News, Radio Five Live
Neil Nightingale	Head of Natural History Unit
Paul Brannan	Deputy Head of News Interactive
Peter Horrocks	Head of Television News
Peter Rippon	Duty Editor, World at One/PM/etc
Phil Harding	Director, English Networks & Nations
Steve Mitchell	Head Of Radio News
Sue Inglish	Head Of Political Programmes
Frances Weil	Editor of News Special Events

Printed in Great Britain
by Amazon.co.uk, Ltd.,
Marston Gate.